SHADES

Sharman Macdonald was born in Glasgow and became an actress after graduating from Edinburgh University. She gave up acting to write. *When I was a Girl I Used to Scream and Shout* (the Bush Theatre, the Edinburgh Festival and the Whitehall Theatre) won her the Evening Standard Award for most promising playwright and a Thames Television Bursary to be writer in residence at the Bush Theatre. Her other work includes the three plays *When We Were Women* (the Cottesloe and the Edinburgh Festival), *The Brave* (the Bush Theatre) and *All Things Nice* (the Royal Court); the novels *The Beast* and *Night, Night,* and a Channel Four film, *Wild Flowers*.

by the same author

WHEN I WAS A GIRL I USED TO SCREAM AND SHOUT
WHEN WE WERE WOMEN
THE BRAVE
ALL THINGS NICE

SHADES

Sharman Macdonald

faber and faber
LONDON · BOSTON

First published in 1992
by Faber and Faber Limited
3 Queen Square London WC1N 3AU

Photoset by Parker Typesetting Service, Leicester
Printed by Clays Ltd, St Ives plc

© Sharman Macdonald, 1992

Sharman Macdonald is hereby identified as the author
of this work in accordance with Section 77 of the
Copyright, Designs and Patents Act 1988.

All rights whatsoever in this play are strictly
reserved and all amateur and professional
applications for permission to perform them must be
made, in advance, to Patricia Macnaughton,
Macnaughton Lowe Representation Limited,
200 Fulham Road, London SW10 9PN

Lines on page 54 from 'The Twelfth of Never',
words by Paul Francis Webster,
music by Jerry Livingston,
© 1956 Frank Music Corporation.

A CIP record for this book is available from the British Library

ISBN 0-571-16884-1

1 3 5 7 9 10 8 6 4 2

To Patricia Macnaughton
with love

CHARACTERS

PEARL	A woman of thirty-eight
ALAN	A boy of ten, Pearl's son
VIOLET	Pearl's mother
CALLUM	Pearl's friend

NOTE

The clapping rhythm referred to in the stage directions is from a rhyming game that girls play in the school playground.

Shades was first performed at the New Victoria Theatre, Woking, Surrey, on 16 June 1992. The cast was as follows:

PEARL	Pauline Collins
ALAN	Ben Chapman
	Matthew Steer
VIOLET	Daphne Oxenford
CALLUM	James Cosmo
Director	Simon Callow
Designer	Christopher Morley
Lighting Designer	Brian Harris

ACT ONE

Clapping rhythm.

Early evening. August.

A large room, high ceilinged, plaster moulding. A dressing-table with a big mirror. A triptych. A gramophone.

A glow of coral colour. A dance dress. Yards of net skirt. Diamantés shimmering. Lying on a bed.

The room is lit by lamps, and the street light coming through the net curtains.

Laughter.

PEARL *in her housecoat, looking out from behind a net curtain. Out of the great big window. Laughing.*

The sound of hands clapping in rhythm.

ALAN *is standing watching his mother.*

ALAN: Nosey, that's you.

PEARL: Don't be cheeky.

ALAN: Nosey parker, that's you.

PEARL: You watch your tongue.

  I'm looking, that's what I'm doing. That's all I'm doing. What harm is there? I'm doing nobody any harm. For God's sake. What's wrong with you? Eh?

ALAN: They'll see you.

PEARL: Is that what's bothering you? Is it? And I thought you had a conscience.

  Don't look like that.

  How'll they see me? They're that wrapped up in themselves, the pair of them. They're not thinking about me. (*Her voice is loud in protest. It's naturally loud, Pearl's voice. When she feels guilty it's louder. Or when she's defending herself, as she is now.*) Come on. Come here. Come and look. Alan. Come on.

ALAN: Sh. Sh. Sh.

PEARL: Don't you shush me.

  They're away across the street, for God's sake. They're not going to hear me.

I

Shushing me. Who do you think you are?

Even if they had their windows open, and who in their right minds would open up their windows on a night like this, they'd not hear me. Come and see. Come on, Alan. (*She reaches out her hand. There's the sound of rain from outside. And a small wind blowing. She's shivering,* PEARL.) Give me a cuddle. Keep me warm. You've got to have a laugh. If we couldn't laugh at ourselves, where would we be? The world would be a sorrier place, and that's a fact. They laugh at us, them over there. I'm damn sure they do. And why the bloody hell not, eh? Why not? You've got to have a sense of humour, Alan.

(*She tugs* ALAN *over to the window. Puts her arms round him. Holds him there.*)

There's a chill this fine evening. You keep me warm, son. Eh? Keep me nice and warm.

Canoodling away, the pair of them. Look. See. Like some honeymoon couple. Fifty if they're a day.

ALAN: I can't see through the rain.

PEARL: Look at that. Did you see? Did you?

And him a newsagent.

(*She digs her fingers into his shoulders.*)

ALAN: Don't.

PEARL: And a member of the Rotary Club.

(ALAN *shrugs her off.*)

ALAN: You're hurting me.

PEARL: Och, you great soft thing.

They should shut the curtain, so they should. (*But she's thrilled by it.*) Mind, I'm glad they don't.

See this window. This is the best window in the whole street. The view from this window. If I was an an old lady, I'd sit here all day long. And I'd dress in black, as befits my widowhood. Respected by all, I'd be. I'd crochet. Can you see me with my crochet, Alan? Can you?

ALAN: You can't crochet.

PEARL: I can learn. You watch your tone of voice. A person could get very hurt by that tone of voice if a person had a mind to.

ALAN: Are you going out or aren't you?

PEARL: It's an education this window. I'd have my crocheting
and a thermos flask of good hot tea. Shawls I'd crochet. I'd
never move. I'd be that happy. I'd be content. I'd not be the
crabbit old thing that some of them are.

ALAN: You're crabbit enough already.

(PEARL *decides to ignore that.*)

PEARL: The things I've seen from this window.
What have we got eh? If we haven't got other people.

ALAN: I'm glad for them.

PEARL: Eh?

ALAN: I think it's nice.

PEARL: What?

ALAN: You know.

PEARL: I don't know. Not till you tell me. 'You know.' (*She turns
away from the window.*) Language is our only means of
communication, Alan. It's to be used properly. Now you tell
me what I don't know.

ALAN: What?

PEARL: Come on.

ALAN: Come on what?

PEARL: 'I think it's nice.' That's what you said. What for God's
sake's 'nice'? What do you think's 'nice'? (*She advances on*
ALAN. *He's laughing at her.*) Come on.

ALAN: Don't get so aerated.

PEARL: What kind of word's that? 'Aerated.' Bread's aerated.

ALAN: You're an embarrassment, do you know that? Don't touch
me, for God's sake. (*He's dodging to the other side of the bed.*)

PEARL: Don't you talk to me like that. Think you're the big man?
Is that what you think? You're that free with your language.

ALAN: Love's nice.

PEARL: Eh? (*An interrogatory noise of stunning length. One* PEARL's
very partial to.)

ALAN: Love.

PEARL: Oh my God. (*She's laughing at him.*)

ALAN: Them two over there.

PEARL: Listen to you.

ALAN: You're supposed to be going out.

PEARL: Love?

ALAN: Yes.

PEARL: Is that right? (*She's got his arm.*)

ALAN: Yes. (*He's laughing.*) What's wrong with that?

PEARL: That's what you think, is it?

ALAN: Are you not going to get ready?

PEARL: Love's nice.

ALAN: Yes.

    (*He knows* PEARL *is going to tickle him.*)

PEARL: What do you know about love? Eh? (*She's got him down on the bed.*) Tell me.

ALAN: You'll be late.

PEARL: What do you know?

ALAN: Stop it. (*He's laughing.*) I love you.

PEARL: You don't get round me like that, and you needn't think it. Love!

ALAN: I do. I do.

PEARL: Down behind the bicycle sheds, eh?

ALAN: No.

PEARL: Don't think I don't know. I'm supposed to close my eyes to all that. Why should I close my eyes? Eh?

ALAN: Stop it.

PEARL: I know what boys get up to.

    You're a right one you.

    I know you.

ALAN: You're going to be late.

PEARL: I'm not going to pretend. And I'm not going to pretend I disapprove either.

ALAN: Mother.

PEARL: I'm no hypocrite.

    (*She's got her hands poised. She's sitting on him so he can't move.*)

ALAN: Don't tickle me.

PEARL: Say 'please'.

ALAN: No.

PEARL: Come on.

ALAN: I won't.

PEARL: 'Please.'

ALAN: I will not.

PEARL: Aye you will.

4

ALAN: No.

PEARL: You will all right.

ALAN: Please. (*He's laughing and laughing. Tired out laughing, though she hasn't touched him yet.*)

PEARL: You can laugh, can you? You can laugh.

ALAN: Don't tickle me. Please.

PEARL: Come here. Come on. Give me a great big hug.

(*She bear-hugs him. They're close to the dress on the bed, the pair of them.*)

Mind my dress.

You watch it with the girls eh? Don't let them get to you. You're o'er young for that.

(*Silence.*)

What are you thinking?

ALAN: Nothing.

PEARL: Aye you are. You are so.

ALAN: I'm not.

PEARL: Tell me.

ALAN: I'm not thinking anything.

PEARL: That's not possible. Human beings think. That's what they do. Nary a moment goes by without them thinking. Much good may it do them. The air's full of thoughts, God help us. I want to know what you're thinking.

ALAN: It's private.

PEARL: What?

I gave birth to you. You grew in my belly. Any thought you have, that belongs to me.

Alan?

(*Pause.*)

If you're like this now, what'll you be like at puberty, eh? I dread to think.

(*She lays her hand on his cheek.*)

You're awful big. Where's the wee thing I gave birth to?

(*She pats his thigh.*)

Great thighs on you, and your great big feet.

(*It's all too sickly for ALAN.*)

ALAN: Eh?

PEARL: Don't say that. Eh? That's the most annoying sound. Eh?

I don't know where you get it from. Pardon, say. Or what.
That's permissible, and perfectly grammatical.
(*She prods the sound at him.*)
Eh? Eh?
There now. (*A quick hug and she lets him go.*)
I'm all hot and sweaty. And I've had my bath and the fire's
not stoked so I'll not get another. Here. (*She gives him a
hairbrush.*) Brush my hair out.
I'll sit quiet.
(*She's at the dressing-table.*)
Come on, son. Brush my hair out for me.
(*Clapping rhythm.*)

(ALAN *takes his mother's hair down. She's had it in pins from her
bath. It goes halfway down her back.*)

PEARL: Your gran's late.

ALAN: Don't go out.

PEARL: When your gran comes.

ALAN: Don't go.

PEARL: You'll be all right with your gran.

ALAN: Why do you have to go out?

PEARL: Are you going to brush my hair? Or are you just going to
stand there?
(*She picks the small mirror up from the dressing-table. Examines
herself in it.*)
Oh God. That face. It's the map of my life, that face.
Crenellated. I've a new line every morning to greet the day.
If only it brought wisdom with it, age. That would be some
compensation. Bye-bye, face. (*She puts the mirror down.*)
You see what I'll bring you when I come back.
Long strokes now.
(*Her hair's hanging down her back.* ALAN's *brushing it, touching
it.*)

ALAN: I like your face.

PEARL: As well somebody does.

ALAN: Callum must. Or he wouldn't go out with you.

PEARL: Don't say his name like that.

ALAN: What?

PEARL: Say it like you like him.

(ALAN *brushes her hair*.)

A menu I'll bring you.

ALAN: I'm not a baby.

(*Pause*.)

PEARL: You've gentle hands. When you grow up to be a man, you keep your gentle hands. A woman likes that. You listen to your old mother. A woman likes a gentle man.

And those wee biscuit things that you get with your coffee at the end. And my napkin. I'll bring you that if I can manage. We could do with some new napkins. Maybe I'll bring them all from our table. And an ashtray. What do you think of that? A posh ashtray that I'll hide in my bag and bring home to you.

(ALAN'*s stopped brushing*.)

Dear God, I'm only going out. I'm allowed to go out.

Come on. You've not finished yet.

You don't get away with it that easily.

ALAN: You've got a white hair.

PEARL: I have not.

ALAN: You have.

PEARL: There's no white hair on my head.

ALAN: There is.

PEARL: You'll not find one.

ALAN: There. It's there.

PEARL: Not on my head.

(*Pause. She's looking at him in the mirror*.)

Pull it out then. Come on. What are you waiting for? Hurry up.

(ALAN *tugs feebly*.)

Harder.

(ALAN *pulls really hard*.)

What do you want? Do you want to pull my head off?

Ah. (*She rubs her head*.)

Where is it?

You haven't lost it. That's my hair. Give it to me.

ALAN: Christ.

(*He gives the hair to her*.)

PEARL: Don't say that. Gives me the shivers, that. You keep your

7

bad language for the playground. I don't want it here.
Oh my God.
(*She stretches the hair out long in her fingers.*)
Come here. Come on.
(ALAN *sits down beside her.*)
Call that white. I can see gold in that. See there, in the light.
Red I can see. Touches of brown, fading in and out. Just
faint. That's not white.

ALAN: It's white all right.

PEARL: Alan.

ALAN: What?
(*Pause.*)
What is it?

PEARL: Am I old?

ALAN: I don't know.

PEARL: What kind of an answer's that? That's no answer to give a
woman of my age when she's sitting in front of a mirror
chasing after her youth that's gone. Lie, why don't you?
There's nothing wrong with a wee white lie when it's told for
kindness sake. I can't be old tonight.
(*Pause.*)
Listen to that rain. I believe it'll thunder.
Was that a car? Was it? Swishing there?
(*Shrugs her shoulders. And back to the mirror.*)
What shall I do with my hair, Alan? Shall I leave it down?
Shall I put it up? Alan?
Have I any more white in there?
(ALAN *goes to look.*)
Never mind. I don't want to know.
Oh God, listen to that rain.
No need to fear the thunder, son. Thunder'll not hurt you.
Your gran'll look after you.
I'll leave it down for now, Alan. What do you think?
Is there any more grey?
Or will I put it up?
(*Clapping rhythm.*)

PEARL: I'm not old.

Tell me I'm pretty. Come on, Alan. You're my man.
'You're a very pretty lady.' Say.

ALAN: Stop it, Mum.

PEARL: Put on the gramophone.

Come on. We'll cheer ourselves up. It's the rain. Draws the
tears out. Makes you maudlin.

(*She laughs.*)

This is not getting me out.

(*Stands. Stretches. Peeps out the window.*)

I've never seen rain like that. Stottin' down it is.

Victor Sylvester we'll have. Alan.

They've shut their curtains. Spoilsports.

You get that gramophone on. None of your highbrow stuff,
now. Victor Sylvester. I've got a sadness on me.

This is not getting me ready.

What's taking you so long?

(ALAN's *got the top of the gramophone up.*)

ALAN: Needs a new needle.

PEARL: There's a packet there, is there not?

ALAN: Yes.

PEARL: Well then? Do you need to be spoonfed?

(*She's pacing now.*)

Oh we're quiet in this house and that's a fact. It's company
we need in this house, and I don't just mean your gran.

We're too much together, you and me.

Do you hear me?

Alan?

ALAN: Yes.

PEARL: What?

ALAN: I hear you. I hear you.

PEARL: Chivvying each other. Morning till night. You and me. I
want us to be friends, Alan.

It's a man I need. And you need a father.

ALAN: Don't start.

PEARL: Well?

ALAN: I've got you.

PEARL: That's not the point.

ALAN: You're all I want.

9

PEARL: You need more than me.

(*She's got her housecoat off. Standing in a strapless silk slip.*)

It's close. And it's damp. And I'm shivering. And I'm hot.

ALAN: You're enough for me.

PEARL: You'll be all grown up soon. Then where'll I be?

ALAN: I'll never leave you.

PEARL: Will you not?

ALAN: I'll always love you.

PEARL: Nonsense.

(*Pause.*)

You get that music on.

(*Victor Sylvester strains through the room.*)

That's better.

We bring children up to let them go. And if they don't go and take their freedom from us we've failed. I'm telling you.

(*She's moving in time with the music. Arms held out.*)

ALAN: I'll choose your necklace.

PEARL: You will. Will you?

ALAN: I'll choose your perfume.

PEARL: You'll not have much to choose from.

ALAN: The gold bottle with the black top.

PEARL: Here.

ALAN: Let me smell.

PEARL: Come here.

(*She opens the bottle and sniffs.*)

There's nothing subtle about this perfume. If you're going to wear scent, you should wear scent. That's what I say. And let the whole world know it.

(*She moves close to him with the bottle.*)

I'll not bite you.

(*She dabs it behind his ears.*)

A right fancy boy. What'll your gran say?

(*Dabs it at his throat.*)

Come on, my fancy man.

(*She puts the bottle down.*)

Come on. (*Opens out her arms.*) Come and dance.

ALAN: I can't dance.

PEARL: Of course you can. Everyone can dance.

ALAN: I can't.

PEARL: No such word.

ALAN: Yes there is.

PEARL: Time you learned then.

Are you angry with me?

ALAN: What do you think?

PEARL: Don't be angry son. I am what I am. That's my cross and
I have to bear it. (*Laughs*.) I'm not so damn bad.

Stand on my feet. I'll dance you.

ALAN: I'm too big.

PEARL: Just this once.

ALAN: I can't.

PEARL: I want to dance.

(*She's imperious standing there, her arms open wide.* ALAN *comes
to her.*)

What was so hard about that?

Put them sideways. They're crushing my toes.

Right.

When did you get to be so big?

Head up.

Ready?

Two three.

You're like a block of wood. Relax.

ALAN: I'm frightened of hurting you.

PEARL: You're not hurting me.

ALAN: I'm frightened I might.

PEARL: Stand down. We'll do it properly.

ALAN: I can't.

PEARL: You can so.

ALAN: How can I?

PEARL: Because I say so.

Right?

A man's firm in the dancing. The man's in charge. Might be
the only time in your life, so make the most of it.

Tell your woman where you want to go.

Get your hand on my back. Don't be afraid. I'll not bite you.
I'm your mother. Higher. Right.

11

Gentle pressure of your hand. Firm, mind. Don't leave her in any doubt.

There's nothing worse than a limp sweaty hand at your back and a man that doesn't know what he's about.

Watch.

(*She leaves him. Twirls.*)

One two three. One two three.

(*Comes back to him. Adjusts his hand.*)

You're leading.

And.

There.

I knew you could.

What did I tell you?

You're a fine dancer.

Never deny your abilities, Alan. False modesty. It's unpleasant to watch and it's a spit in the eye of God that gave you the talent in the first place.

No trouble at all.

(*Holds him there.*

And the music fades down until it's the merest whisper. Ghost soft.

They're caught in the light, the pair of them.)

PEARL: What are you thinking now? Right now?

Alan? How dare you have thoughts that I don't know?

I wish you talked more. Alan?

Maybe if I talked less.

Alan.

What are you thinking?

(*Music up.*)

Oh God. (*She's rubbing her foot.*)

ALAN: Sorry.

PEARL: Oh my God.

ALAN: I didn't mean . . .

PEARL: You clumsy big oaf.

ALAN: Sorry.

PEARL: If you knew what I suffered with my feet. Chilblains I've got.

ALAN: I didn't mean . . .

PEARL: Corns.

ALAN: Mother.

PEARL: The fortune I spend at the chiropodist.

ALAN: Sorry.

PEARL: That's just a word. It doesn't make things better.
Take that look off your face.

ALAN: I'm sorry.

PEARL: It's not the end of the world.
Turn that damn thing off. And don't scratch the record.
(*She's still rubbing her foot.*)
What's the time? What time is it?
It's late, isn't it?
(*She stretches out her foot.*)
I've your grandmother's feet, more's the pity. Your
grandfather now, he had lovely feet.
(*The music's off.*)
That's better.
(*She's peering at her wristwatch.*)
You father hated my feet. Do you know that? That always
hurt me. What right did he have to hate my feet? And the
more he teased me about them the more I longed for some
man to come along and hold them in his hands and kiss my
toes, each and every one. Corns and all. I didn't care who.
Why could he not love my feet? Never love 'in spite of',
Alan. For that's no love at all.
This clockface is far too small. Fancy making a thing this
size.
You've young eyes. What's the time?
What time is it? (*She stretches out her wrist.*)
Oh God I'm cold.

ALAN: Half past seven.

PEARL: Is it?

ALAN: Twenty-five past.

PEARL: Is it?
I can't see to thread a needle now.
Where's your gran?
Your gran should be here.
(*She's at the window again. Putting the perfume on. Throwing*

back her head and letting it run down the line of her neck.)
Nuit d'or. This perfume's called. That's French. Night of gold. You'll be doing French next year. See and you work hard. And you'll be able to go to foreign lands. And you'll be able to talk to them. That's a great thing. I can't do that. You be better than me, do you hear?
Nuit d'or. Say it after me. *Nuit d'or*. Say it.

ALAN: *Nuit d'or*.

PEARL: There. There now. Now you know some French.
I can't see her.
That's what I want for you. The world at your feet. That you can pick and choose from. All the mysteries of the big wide world. That you can do what you want with. As long as you're good. You'll not suffer if you're good.
What time is it? What time does it say now?
(ALAN *comes to the window by her.* PEARL *touches his hair.*)
Oh God, Alan, don't you be like me. Thank God you're not a girl. I couldn't stand that. Watching a girl grow up. Watching her become more and more like me as the years went on. Wanting her to be like me. Hating her for it. Knowing her through and through. Hating her for that too. Don't you ever be like me.

ALAN: I'm quite safe.

PEARL: What?

ALAN: Mother?

PEARL: When you were inside me. I prayed for you not to be a girl. On my knees I prayed.
(*Pause.*)
Don't mind me. Pay me no mind.

ALAN: I don't.

PEARL: That's all right then.
(*She looks at him.*)
Is it time to put my dress on? It must be that time at the very least.

ALAN: Don't go.
(*Clapping rhythm.*)

ALAN: I don't want you to go.

PEARL: Don't be silly.

ALAN: I don't like him.

PEARL: Yes you do.

ALAN: Him looking at you.

PEARL: Don't be ridiculous.
      He's got to look at me. What's he supposed to do, eh?
      I won't have this.

ALAN: Right.

PEARL: Less of your nonsense.

ALAN: All right!
      (*Pause.*)

PEARL: How does he look at me?

ALAN: Mother.

PEARL: I want to know.
      (*Wheedling.*)
      Alan.
      Come on.
      Tell me.

ALAN: What?

PEARL: How he looks at me.
      Tell me.
      Please, Alan. How?

ALAN: Up and down.

PEARL: What?

ALAN: All over.

PEARL: Eh?

ALAN: Every part of you.

PEARL: Does he? (*She's pleased.*)

ALAN: You're pathetic.

PEARL: Don't you speak to me like that.

ALAN: The cat that got the cream.

ALAN: I am not.

ALAN: Look at you.

PEARL: What?

ALAN: You think you're great.

PEARL: I do not.

ALAN: Aye you do.

PEARL: Men and women, Alan.

ALAN: It's going to thunder.

PEARL: One day you'll be a man.

ALAN: If I don't die first.

PEARL: Don't say that. That's an awful thing to say. That's asking
for it. Do you hear me? Never say a thing like that or God'll
reach down from heaven and smite you where you stand.
You'll be a man. And you'll be a good man, or I'll know the
reason why.
And you'll treat the women right. I'll make sure of that. It's a
mother that teaches her son about women, if she's got the
courage. There'll be plenty of women. You wait. We've a duty
to womankind, we mothers. Plenty women. You'll see.
You're a handsome lad. The women'll be flocking round. Bees
to a honeypot. You wait and see. And you'll want to keep them
there. Oh, I know you don't see that now. Talk, that's what
keeps a woman. I've watched ugly men charm the pants off a
woman. And I mean that. Just by the words that come out of
their mouths. You mind that. Looks, just plain looks, are
nothing without there's something behind them. And I like a
good-looking man. I like a handsome man all right. I'm a
softie me. A man looks into my eyes and I go weak at the
knees. But I recover quick enough, believe you me. Cherish
her. You don't suffocate her – mind that now. Leave her her
freedom. Looks are nothing with no thought behind them.

ALAN: I don't like thunder. I'll never marry.

PEARL: You'll have your woman. I'll be an old lady then. I'll not be
so very lovely. You'll not think so. And neither will I. I'll be
old, and I'll hold your babies in my arms. For you'll marry
some nice girl that I can get on with. Won't you, Alan. And I'll
be an old grandmother. That'll be a relief. I'll not need to worry
then. My worrying days'll be done. Funny old thing I'll be.

ALAN: Are you going out?

PEARL: What?

ALAN: Get a move on.

(*Clapping rhythm.*)

(*Thunder.*)

ALAN: Listen.

16

PEARL: You'll have to fasten this up for me.

ALAN: I don't like the thunder.

PEARL: Don't be such a baby.

(*She's at the bed. At the dress.*)

Is that a mark?

ALAN: Are you going to leave me?

PEARL: Don't tell me there's a mark on it.

ALAN: Don't leave me.

PEARL: What age are you?

ALAN: Listen.

PEARL: Oh my God, would you look at that? (*She's brushing at it.*)

Go and get some water.

ALAN: Where from?

PEARL: Where do you think? From the tap, for God's sake.

ALAN: What tap?

PEARL: The nearest one. (*She looks at him.*)

ALAN: You go.

PEARL: I'm asking you.

Get the water from the bathroom. Use your brain. What do you think God gave it to you for?

ALAN: What'll I put it in? The water?

PEARL: Use your initiative, for God's sake. Alan. I've a mark on this dress. You'd not have me going out looking like an old tramp. Looking like a streetwalker, for God's sake. You want me to do you credit, don't you?

ALAN: It's raining.

PEARL: Not in the bathroom.

ALAN: It'll get all marked by the rain. Won't it? Anyway.

PEARL: Are you going to get that water?

ALAN: No.

PEARL: Do you think I'm going out without a coat? Do you? I'll have my coat on, for God's sake. My coat'll keep the dress covered. My good coat and my umbrella. I'll have that too. And I'll be in his car.

ALAN: You'll be in his car?

PEARL: Of course I will.

ALAN: You won't need an umbrella then, will you?

PEARL: I've a mark on this dress. It should have gone to the

17

dry-cleaners, this dress. I should have had a new dress, for God's sake. Are you going to get me that water or are you not?

ALAN: I'm not.

PEARL: What're you frightened of?

ALAN: What're you frightened of?

PEARL: I wish your gran would come. Get it for me.

ALAN: You're scared of going out.

PEARL: Don't be daft.

ALAN: You're petrified.

(*Pause.*)

PEARL: What the hell do you mean by that?

ALAN: Look at you.

(*Pause.*)

PEARL: You'll not even do a simple thing for me?

(*She leaves the room.*

Her voice comes back to him.)

I clothe you. I care for you and all that that entails. The sacrifices I've made for you.

(ALAN *goes over to the bed, touches the net of the skirt.*)

They've all seen that dress.

(ALAN *picks up the dress. Holds it gently to him.*)

The times I've worn that.

(ALAN *is cradling the dress. Swaying to and fro.*)

I had that dress when you father was alive.

(ALAN *is smelling the dress.*

He's still holding it when PEARL *comes back in. Quietly. Watches him. She's holding the water.*)

PEARL: A wee bit thunder won't harm you.

ALAN: I know.

PEARL: Are you trying to strangle that?

ALAN: Smells of you.

PEARL: Oh God.

ALAN: What?

(PEARL *sniffs at it.*)

PEARL: I can't smell anything.

ALAN: That's because you smell of you.

PEARL: I do not.

ALAN: You're used to it.

PEARL: Are you saying I smell?

ALAN: Everyone does.

PEARL: I've just had a bath. Duck's disease, that's your trouble. Nose too close to your own backside.

ALAN: It's nice.

PEARL: Eh?

ALAN: It smells nice.

PEARL: How can a smell be nice? A smell? A perfume's nice. A scent's nice. A smell. Dogs smell.

(ALAN's *watching her*.)

ALAN: You can go if you want to.

PEARL: You give me your permission, do you?

ALAN: If you like.

PEARL: That's big of you.

ALAN: I'm just saying.

PEARL: Sit down on the bed. Hold me out that mark.

ALAN: Mother.

PEARL: You think I need your permission, do you?
We're in each other's pockets you and me.
I'll rub. You hold.
Stretch it out tight.
It's gravy that. That's what that looks like. Or soup.

ALAN: What kind of soup?

PEARL: How should I know what kind of soup? What sort of a question's that?

ALAN: You're a mucky eater.

PEARL: I beg your pardon?

ALAN: You're always in a hurry.

PEARL: If I'm in a hurry, you're what I'm in a hurry for.
You think you're my keeper.
I'm the parent here.
You're not my keeper. Much as I love you. I'm my own woman. I grew up a long time ago.

ALAN: We take care of each other, you and me.

PEARL: Och, your face and parsley. You're letting that sag.

ALAN: Why are you frightened of going out?

PEARL: We'll put the electric bar fire on for it to dry.

A long time ago. I grew up. Do you hear me?

ALAN: Why are you frightened?

PEARL: I'm not.

ALAN: You always are.

PEARL: I'm not frightened.

(ALAN *strokes her bare shoulder*.)

ALAN: You've lovely skin.

PEARL: Get your hand off. (*She laughs*.) Stop pawing me.

(*She puts the fire on.*
Clapping rhythm.)

PEARL: Come down here. Come on. Come down.

(ALAN *tries to pick the dress up and hold the wet bit out at the*
same time.)

Mind what you're doing.

ALAN: I'll probably wet the bed.

(PEARL *helps him*.)

PEARL: So you probably will. Hold it out to the fire.

ALAN: Gran'll be angry with me.

PEARL: I'll be angry with you. Your gran doesn't have to wash the
sheets.

ALAN: She'll still be angry.

PEARL: You could try not to wet the bed.

ALAN: It's raining.

PEARL: So what?

ALAN: All the water's running down the roof. I hear it in my
sleep. I dream of waterfalls.

PEARL: Well don't.

ALAN: I can't help my dreams.

PEARL: Try.

ALAN: Or fountains I dream of. Gushing. I always wet the bed
when it rains and the water's running down the roof.

PEARL: You wet your bed. Do you hear me? You can strip it your
own self. You wet it. You strip it. Are you listening to me? I
don't care what time of night it is. And you can wash your
own sheets.

(*She stretches out the dress.*)

Has that stain gone? Can you see.

20

ALAN: Don't know.

PEARL: Eh?

ALAN: It's wet.

PEARL: I'm never going to be ready.

(*She just sits there. Looking into the bar fire.*)

Dream about rugby why don't you? Scoring a try.

ALAN: No.

PEARL: Why not?

ALAN: I play it, don't I?

PEARL: You like it.

ALAN: Why do I have to dream about it?

PEARL: You don't have to. You don't have to dream about
anything. Don't you fire up like that. You like rugby.

ALAN: No I don't.

PEARL: You do so.

ALAN: I do not.

PEARL: Since when?

ALAN: Ages.

PEARL: You're good at rugby.

ALAN: I don't have to like it just because I'm good at it. Do I?

PEARL: It helps.

ALAN: Do I?

PEARL: I always like the things I'm good at.

ALAN: What are you good at?

PEARL: Eh?

ALAN: Come on.

Tell me.

What the hell are you good at?

PEARL: Don't you swear at me.

ALAN: Tell me what you're good at.

PEARL: Alan.

ALAN: Eh?

PEARL: I'm warning you.

ALAN: Eh?

PEARL: You heard.

ALAN: Jesus Christ.

(PEARL *slaps him hard.*)

PEARL: Don't you take the name of the Lord thy God in vain.

Don't you.

(*Pause.*)

ALAN: You're a bitch.

(PEARL *slaps him again.*

Pause.

PEARL's *shaking.*)

PEARL: Am I to come in to change the sheets?

ALAN: You hurt me.

PEARL: And I'll hurt you again if I have to.

ALAN: Why?

PEARL: I'll get in. It'll be past midnight when I get in. Don't have me change the sheets. I've my work in the morning. I don't go out often, Alan. It's a rare thing for me to go out.

ALAN: You don't love me.

You don't even like me.

You think you're so great with your boyfriend, the big souk. Swanking about, the pair of you. And your dress. Everybody's laughing at you. You're too old to wear your hair down your back. You're ugly with your hair like that. I see them. You walking down the street on his arm. They're all laughing and they're nodding their heads.

PEARL: You'll get another one . . .

You mind your mouth.

ALAN: You're scared to go out.

PEARL: Tie my hair back for me, Alan. I've got a ribbon. You tie it back in a good velvet bow. You tie a nice bow. It takes a man to tie a ribbon. That's what my father said. Takes a sailor to tie a ribbon.

ALAN: You're always scared.

PEARL: My father always tied my bows for me.

ALAN: Why are you? Why are you scared?

(*Pause.*)

PEARL: I'm a baby. Right?

Come here. Come close. Come on. I'm sorry I hit you. You asked for it, mind. Come on. Come here.

I'm a baby and I'm looking up at my mother. I'm lying in her arms looking up. And I'm thinking, is this all I get?

ALAN: You can't remember that.

22

PEARL: Aye I can. I can remember everything. I can remember
back to my pram and beyond. That's my curse. And your
gran's too. Doesn't make her life any too comfortable.
Her big face looking down at me. Big cross face. She was
always angry, my mother. Still is. And I open my mouth and
I bawl my lungs out. For I want more.
I'm in here and I'm looking out my window and the world's
shining. What I expect when I go out . . .
You've got to grab on to life. Grab and hold hard.
Before it slips away . . .
What do you think? Do you think there's more to have? For
I do. I think there's a whole lot more. And what if I don't
find it?

ALAN: Take me away from that school.

PEARL: Sometimes I'm filled with hope. I'm so full of hope I
tremble for the passion of it. So I'm scared. I'm scared right
enough.
Eh?

ALAN: I hate that school.

PEARL: Tie me a bow in my hair.
(*She fetches a black bow from the dressing-table. A velvet one.
Kneels down by* ALAN *at the fire. Gives him the ribbon.*)
I pay for your education. Don't you throw it back in my face.

ALAN: Please, Mother.
(*He's gathering her hair back. Putting the ribbon round it.*)

PEARL: That school makes you special. That school sets you apart.

ALAN: I don't want . . .

PEARL: Makes you one of the chosen.

ALAN: My friends . . .

PEARL: If I could afford it I'd send you to Eton. Do you hear me?
We could have a better life if I didn't pay for your education.

ALAN: Take me away from that school.

PEARL: We could have holidays abroad.

ALAN: Take me away from it.

PEARL: Why?

ALAN: I want to be like the others.

PEARL: Don't be ridiculous.
What for? What on earth for?

It's one of my triumphs that I've got you at that school.
You've got to count your triumphs and hold them every one.
(*She looks at him.*)
You like it, don't you. You like that school. That was your
father's school.
(ALAN'*s defeated.*)

ALAN: Yes.

PEARL: I didn't hear you.

ALAN: Yes. Yes I like it.

PEARL: Make the best of it, then. That's all I ask.
Are you done?
(*She feels the bow at the back of her head.*
She's startled.)
Was that a knock at the door?

ALAN: What would she knock for?

PEARL: Was it? (*She rushes to the window.*)

ALAN: She'd ring the bell.

PEARL: Don't get that dress too near the fire.

ALAN: She'd ring it loud and long.

PEARL: No one there.

ALAN: That's my gran for you. Always has to announce herself.
'Here I am. Here I'm here.' Rrrrrring.

PEARL: Don't burn that dress.
(*Clapping rhythm.*)

ALAN: Did you think it might be him?

PEARL: Better not be.
Don't get it too near.
(*She's still at the window.*)
All the curtains are shut now. All along the street.
(*She shivers.*)
It's cold.

ALAN: Tisn't.

PEARL: Something walked over my grave.

ALAN: I'd probably kill myself if I didn't have you. (*Very factual this.*)

PEARL: Eh?

ALAN: When you die, I'll die too.

PEARL: What for?

24

ALAN: I wouldn't want to be here without you. Wouldn't be any
    fun.
PEARL: I'm not planning to go yet. When I do, I'll let you know.
ALAN: Come down by the fire. I'll give you a cuddle.
PEARL: Maybe they've gone to bed. Eh? That pair over there.
    What do you think?
ALAN: I'll keep you warm.
PEARL: You'll burn that.
ALAN: I won't.
PEARL: I'm telling you.
ALAN: I will not.
PEARL: It'll be winter soon and we'll be all shut in. Feel that chill.
ALAN: Come down beside me.
PEARL: I hate August. The end of all things, August. Never
    becoming. Always become. Dirty August. Plants all tired
    out. Breathless in the heat. And that chill right on the top of
    the air. Neither summer nor yet autumn either.
    I hate the winter. You have to be still in winter. I can't be
    still. Oh God, I won't be still.
    (*A flash of lightning.*)
    Count, come on. One two three four five. (*Then the thunder
    comes.*) You didn't count.
    (*It's a lively memory this next. She enjoys it.*)
    When I was wee we'd sit at the window, all the lot of us. And
    I'd have Billy on my knee. And he was always scratching at
    his eczema. Scratching till his scabs bled. A right wee fidget.
    He'd rub at his eyes, Billy, till they rolled right back in his
    head. The winge that he was. Whining and whining. Though
    you'd not think it to look at him now. Great big man he is
    now. Always a joke on his lips. Though I question the taste
    of some of them. I like clean humour. There's many that
    think it's clever to be dirty. I'm not one of them. He's a one,
    your Uncle Billy. And he'd pull my hair sitting on my knee
    there, tyke that he was. And we'd count for the miles.
    Looking out the window in the dark.
    (*Flash.*)
    There's another one. One two three four. (*Thunder.*) It's
    moving in on us.

Where is she? Your gran?
My God, I'm chilled to the bone. (*She's looking out the window again.*) There's sweat on my hands and I'm freezing. There's a light in that bedroom now. They've got the curtains open just a crack. That's where they are. That's where they are all right.
(*Clapping rhythm.*)

ALAN: What about your make-up?

PEARL: Eh?

ALAN: Are you not putting on any lipstick? You look ill without lipstick.

PEARL: Oh my God. (*She whisks round to the dressing-table.*) What can I be thinking of?
Look at that face. I can't go out with a face like that. That's naked, that face. That's a terrible face. That's tragic. We'll paint a smile on it. Eh? Will we?

ALAN: Tell me about Daddy.

PEARL: Not tonight.

ALAN: Please.

PEARL: I've a lipstick here that'll match that dress exactly. Would that be too much? What do you think?

ALAN: It's horrible.

PEARL: Is it?

ALAN: It's as well one of us has got taste.

PEARL: Maybe you're right.

ALAN: A story about Daddy.
(*PEARL discards the lipstick.*)

PEARL: What would I do without you?

ALAN: Please.

PEARL: You keep me together and no mistake.

ALAN: One story.

PEARL: I'm going out with Callum. I'll not have your father's ghost out with me to keep me company.

ALAN: A funny story.

PEARL: How's that?
(*She purses her lips at him. Blows a kiss.*)

ALAN: Do your eyebrows like Joan Crawford.

(PEARL *draws them in very carefully*.)

I like a woman with a strong face. I like a handsome woman.

PEARL: Do you now?

ALAN: I do.

PEARL: I like a man that knows what he likes.

ALAN: Eyeshadow.

PEARL: Blue or green?

ALAN: Blue.

PEARL: I've gold here. 'Shimmer of moondust.' That's what it's called. Charm him with the magic of the night sky. What do you think?

ALAN: Don't be cheap.

PEARL: Blue then.

(*She puts on the blue*.)

Am I not a beauty?

ALAN: Your nose is shining.

PEARL: I'm not using powder.

ALAN: Everybody does.

PEARL: I don't have to do a thing just because everybody does it. I'm my own person. I'll be different if I want.

ALAN: You look common with your nose shining.

PEARL: Clogs up the pores.

ALAN: Suit yourself.

PEARL: I don't mind adding sparkle. A bit of colour. Brighten up a dull day.

Rouge I'll have.

ALAN: If you want to look like a china doll.

(PEARL *puts the rouge down*.)

PEARL: You're a puritan, do you know that?

ALAN: Tell me a story.

PEARL: Will it make you feel better?

(*She's licking at a brush and rubbing it into a block mascara. Brushing at her eyelashes.* ALAN's *sitting beside her on the dressing-table stool – it's a long one – so that they're both reflected in the great big dressing-table mirror*.)

ALAN: What are those holes all over your nose. And there's wee black bits in them. And there's some on your chin.

PEARL: Oh God.

27

ALAN: Well?

PEARL: Open pores.

ALAN: That's not very nice. You look like you're starting a beard.
Powder'll cover that.

(PEARL *powders her nose and her chin.*)

PEARL: You know what you want, don't you?
And you make damn sure you get it.
My hands are numb. Cold as death, my hands. Feel.
(*She sticks them down his back.* ALAN *screams.*)
Mind that dress.
(ALAN *goes back to the fire.*)

ALAN: The story.
Go on.

PEARL: Your father and me . . .

ALAN: Wait a minute.
(*He pats the floor beside him.* PEARL *comes over, sits down. He coories into her.*)

PEARL: Before you were thought of – before we were wed even –
your father and me, we used to take Mrs Smith's dog for a
walk. Her that always had the Great Danes. Sad things Great
Danes, with their small hearts and their great big bodies and
their short lives. Still, it outlived your father. It was here on
this earth when your father was gone from it, and that's a
fact. King was its name, though he's dead now right enough.
Smelly thing he was, though your father was fond of him.
Out on to the moors we'd go. And I'd love it for the open air.
Even the rain I liked. And your father and me with our
gloves on. Old brown leather gloves he had, with a yellow
lining. I loved these gloves. Curled up at the wrist they were,
for the leather had shrunk they'd been wet that often.

ALAN: Get them out.

PEARL: What?

ALAN: Go on.

PEARL: Get them yourself. I'm not your servant.
(ALAN *gets the gloves from the dressing-table drawer. Gives them
to her.*)
They were good gloves these gloves. Aye, there's wear in
them yet.

28

(*She puts one on. Silence.* ALAN *watches her.*)

ALAN: I'm here. (*He's calling her back. Angrily.*)

PEARL: What?

ALAN: I'm here now.

(*Urgently, he's calling her.*)

PEARL: So you are.

ALAN: Then what happened?

PEARL: Eh?

ALAN: My dad and the dog. (*Impatiently.*) King. The dog.

(*Pause.*)

PEARL: We came to a stream. Now usually this stream, it's the merest trickle. It had been raining though, and the stream's turned into this torrent. Brown and brackish and muddy it was.

ALAN: You're exaggerating.

PEARL: I am not.

ALAN: It wasn't a torrent.

PEARL: How do you know? Were you there? Were you?

ALAN: Exaggerating's a kind of a lie.

PEARL: You tell the story.

ALAN: Not a torrent.

PEARL: Near enough, if I want it to be.

(*She looks at him.* ALAN *subsides.*)

And I've got a new pair of shoes on. And nylons without a run in. And we're standing there contemplating the water. Me and your dad and King the dog. Bloody dog. And I wait for your father to carry me across.

(*Pause.*)

ALAN: Well.

PEARL: I'd be waiting yet.

ALAN: So?

PEARL: He picked up the dog.

Carried the dog across.

ALAN: I bet you gave him what for.

PEARL: Stood there waiting for me. On the other side.

'I haven't got all day,' he said. Looking at me. Him and that dog.

ALAN: I bet he got the worst word in your mouth.

29

PEARL: I couldn't stop laughing. I couldn't get across the stream for laughing. Stuck right in the middle I was. With the water swirling round my ankles.
(*She's laughing now.*)
Alan. The ruination of a good pair of shoes.
Oh God.
(*She looks at her hand with the glove on it. And she's thinking. Takes the glove off. The laughter's stopped.*)
Here.
(*She passes the gloves to* ALAN.)
My nails are all right.
I'm not painting my toenails. That's asking too much.
They'll be inside my shoes.
(*Her leg's stretched out. Toe pointed.*)
I've cut myself shaving.
(*She licks her finger.*)
I've a good pair of legs.
(*Rubs at a bit of blood on her leg.*)
Where's the summer gone?
Get me my stockings.

ALAN: I'm not your servant.
(*He's got the gloves in his hand. The pair. Smoothing them out against his knee.*)

PEARL: Is that a fact? (*She lets him away with it.*)
Your father. I was eight-months pregnant with you and he had me pushing a jeep out of a ditch. That bloody jeep. Weighed a ton. And him at the wheel. He wasn't a small man, your father. And me with my great big belly. You were a nine-pound baby. I was that sick of carrying you around by that time I'd have shoved twenty jeeps out of twenty ditches if I'd thought it would get you started. But you've got a mind of your own. You had then and you have now. See and keep it, son. There's nothing more precious. I thought I'd never get my figure back again. And the varicose veins I had.
(*She stands. Turns to and fro. Stretches her arms up into the air.*)
And piles. I had piles.
(*Gets her stockings out of the drawer. Pushes her hands into them. Examines them for rips.*)

30

But for your school fees, I'd have had a new pair of nylons.
(ALAN *watches her. They weigh each other up, the pair of them.
On the question of schools. They each let it pass.*)
He reminds me of Anthony Eden. Callum does. He's got
class. What do you think? He's a handsome man. Or
Mountbatten. I'd have been a better wife for Mountbatten
than that one he's landed himself with. Pity I move in the
wrong circles.

ALAN: You're a snob.

PEARL: There's not a damn thing wrong with that.
Eh?
His shoulders bear a mighty burden. Anthony Eden.
(*Examining the stockings for rips all the while.*)
I don't vote. I never have and I never will. I don't care what
party they come from. Word games, that's what they play,
and I'll have none of them. You get out there, Alan. You'll
have your education. You'll go to the university, I'll see to
that. You get out there and be an honest man. Sex-daft,
that's what they are, politicians. Dirty men. Or they're fat.
They've all got mistresses and wee flats to keep them in. Sex.
That's all they're in it for. They're rich, and the rich can't be
good. That's what I say. There's too much to tempt them. I
wouldn't want to be rich. I'd like a bit more than I've got
now and no mistake. Comfortable, that's what I'd like to be.
Not rich.
And then I think, 'comfortable' – that 's an awful word.
There's no adventure in 'comfortable'.

ALAN: 'Poor' 's a worse word.

PEARL: You be a politician.
(*One stocking's on.*)
Who do you think he looks like?

ALAN: Who?

PEARL: Who do you think?

ALAN: I don't know.

PEARL: Callum.

ALAN: I don't know.

PEARL: You don't know much.

ALAN: Will you . . . ?

PEARL: Eh?

ALAN: Mother?

PEARL: Will I what?

(*She's not looking at him.*)

Damn. (*She's got the other stocking over her toe.*) Look at that.
Is that not always the way?

ALAN: It's ripped.

PEARL: I can see that. A bit nail varnish. Eh? Callum?

(*She's talking to* ALAN. *They both realize what she's said.*)

Alan. Stop it running.

(*She pulls the stocking up her leg. Fastens the suspenders.
Undoes the nail-varnish bottle.*)

ALAN: Will you marry him?

(PEARL *tends to the stocking. Doesn't look at him.*)

Will you?

PEARL: Maybe. I don't know. And that's the God's honest truth.
And he hasn't asked me.

(*Bright and breezy, she spins them both off into a change of
subject.*)

Democracy. Eh? No one asks me. It's not much I'm asked.
I'd fight no wars. Nothing's worth a man's life, Alan. That's
what I'd tell them.

ALAN: You've got to have wars.

PEARL: Admit that a thing's possible and then God curse it for it's
got to be.

ALAN: You've got to have a war to fix things.

PEARL: I didn't give birth to you for you to go off and get killed.
The waste of time that would be.

Nothing's worth a war.

Is that what they teach you at that school of yours? If that's
what they teach you I'll take you away. I'll take you away all
right.

Put those gloves back so I know where they are.

ALAN: Can I put them under my pillow.

PEARL: Why don't you?

ALAN: For tonight.

PEARL: Good idea.

(ALAN *puts them under the pillow on the bed.*)

32

PEARL: That's not your bed.

ALAN: It hasn't thundered for a while.

PEARL: You just curb your warlike tendencies. Use your brain not your brawn. Do you hear me?

ALAN: It hasn't, has it?

PEARL: We're in the eye of the storm.

I get very lonely sometimes.

ALAN: You've got me.

PEARL: Still.

ALAN: We're all right together.

(PEARL's *powdering under her arms.*)

PEARL: You'll not stay with me all your life. And I wouldn't want you to.

ALAN: It's very quiet.

PEARL: You'll not want to.

ALAN: The wind's gone.

PEARL: Will you?

ALAN: I can't hear the rain.

PEARL: You're off with your friends now, and so you should be. You'll not want me.

ALAN: Your dress is dry.

PEARL: Alan?

ALAN: The stillness. I hate it.

(*Sings.*)

Lu la lu la lu la lu la bye bye.

(*Speaks.*)

Sing me.

(*Sings.*)

Does he want the moon to play with?

(*Speaks.*)

My song.

(*Sings.*)

The stars to run away with?

PEARL: He's a nice man.

ALAN: My song.

(PEARL *sings.*)

PEARL: They'll come if you don't cry.

(*Clapping rhythm.*)

(*She lifts the dress up,* PEARL. *Shakes it. Throws it over her head. Holds it up around her. It's a two-people dress, a strapless number – if she lets it go to fasten it up, it'll fall down.*)

PEARL: Fasten me up, can you?

ALAN: You don't love him.

PEARL: What's love got to do with it? Fasten me up, can you not?

ALAN: Mother.

PEARL: What does it mean? Love. What do you think that means to me? Love? I loved your father, and where did that get me? Oh, I know you're here. Ten years old and what do you know? Nothing. I'm telling you. And God in heaven what am I teaching you? Love? You wait till you're my age and you've been disappointed. Love. I loved your father, that's who I loved. And you look where that's got me. Love. I'll settle for something else. Maybe I will. Maybe I will. Thank you very much. Like all these politicians in that big Whitehall. Compromise. The dirtiest word in the English language. I'll settle for that. Maybe I will. I've had it for love.

ALAN: You love me.

PEARL: Fasten me up.

ALAN: Mother.

PEARL: If I cry. If I do that. I'll kill you whether I love you or not. My make-up'll spoil. My eyes'll be red. A raddled old whore I'll look. A fine sight for a romantic night out. A fine companion.
Yes I said whore.
(*She's furious, and the fury builds.*)
Maybe I do love him. Maybe I do.
This is no kind of childhood for you.
(*Thunder.*)
God damn that thunder, it makes my head ache. And I'm not dressed.

ALAN: Sorry.

PEARL: What for?

ALAN: Sorry.

PEARL: What does that mean? Sorry. We're all sorry. Doesn't mend things. Sorry. A more useless word.

34

Are you going to fasten this dress for me or do I go out in that
street and yell for Mrs Prescott to come and do it for me?

ALAN: You can't marry a man you don't love.

PEARL: I can do anything I want.

(*Pause.*)

Fasten my dress, son. I can't reach round my back and hold
the damn thing up at the same time. I'd have to be a
contortionist to do that.

(*Pause.*)

I'm going out, son. For the evening. That's all. I'm going to
dance. I'm going to laugh a bit. Maybe I'll have a drink.
Maybe I'll smoke a cigarette after the toast to the Queen. I'll
eat and I'll talk. Then I'll come back to you. Exactly the
same person that went out.

Maybe I love him. Maybe I love him after all.

I can't stand here all night.

(*There's a flash.* ALAN *runs over to her. Fastens some of the
dress. The thunder rolls and rolls.* ALAN's *round whimpering in
her arms.*)

It's not the sort of night that makes you rush to get
anywhere.

(*Another flash.*)

My God, that was close. (*She shouts out the window up to the
sky.*) Are you having fun up there? Are you? I hope you are,
for you're making things very difficult for me down here.
Not that you care. A night out. That's all. A night out. My
God, the expectation's going to kill me.

Will we have a treat at the weekend? What do you think?
Will we go to the pictures? And will we have our tea in the
cafeteria? It could be just you and me if you want. Or you
can take a friend. Whatever you like, son. Your treat.

(*She's smoothing the hair back from his face. Wiping the tears
away.*)

We used to do that every Saturday night, your father and me
and your gran looked after you.

You be my best beau, eh? Will we do that, Alan?

Don't you cry on my dress.

A wee bit thunder.

35

You can sleep in here tonight. Get Gran to tuck you up. Leave
the light on. Read yourself to sleep. We'll not bother about the
electric bill for this once. And I'll get in beside you when I get
back. What do you think? And I'll tell you all about it. And I'll
cuddle you.

Do you think he'll bring me a flower?

I'll come back and I'll unpin my flower. And I'll lay it at the
side of the bed. Maybe even on the pillow. And we'll have the
scent of a flower in the room to keep us company while we sleep.
What could be better, eh? And biscuits you'll have that I'll
bring you. Don't forget. Wee sweet biscuits for a midnight feast.
Get your gran to tuck you up in here.

ALAN: I don't like Gran.

PEARL: I'm going out.

ALAN: I don't like her.

PEARL: I'm going out, son.

ALAN: Please.

PEARL: I'd rather have an evening with my feet up, but I'm going
out. It's not very often that I go.

ALAN: She's bad-tempered.

PEARL: Your grandmother . . .

You're making me feel guilty, and I'm damn well letting you.
Stop possessing me. I'm just going out. You're not my
husband. Alan. I'm going out. That's all. An evening out.
God.

Your grandmother means well.

ALAN: How do you know?

PEARL: She loves you.

ALAN: What does that mean?

PEARL: Alan, she's my mother.

Alan, please.

(*She's finished fastening the dress by herself.*)

ALAN: You look lovely.

PEARL: I do, don't I?

(*Pause. She's got her watch at her ear.*)

A more useless. My Father gave me this for my twenty-first
birthday. Your gran nearly leathered him for spending all that
money.

(*She's at the window.*)

Where is she?

For God's sake.

She's late.

Are my seams straight?

They've come downstairs again. Lights burning all over the house. The bills they must have. Whatever they did up there it didn't put them to sleep. Too early in the evening I suppose. What did they bother going upstairs for?

Are they straight?

ALAN: Yes.

PEARL: I had a dance for my twenty-first birthday party.

ALAN: You're a peeping Tom.

PEARL: Do you know the facts of life?

ALAN: The police could get you.

PEARL: I'm not doing any harm.

ALAN: It's against the law.

PEARL: Do you?

ALAN: Yes.

PEARL: I didn't tell you.

ALAN: You didn't have to.

PEARL: Are you sure you've got it right?

ALAN: Yes.

PEARL: As long as you're sure.

ALAN: Mother.

PEARL: What are they burning the lights for if they don't want people to see?

ALAN: I don't know.

PEARL: There you are then.

(*She puts her hand up to her neck.*)

My neck's awful bare.

I had a lilac dress all the way down to the floor for my twenty-first birthday. It's not an easy colour to wear, lilac. Some consider it ageing. But I could wear it. I loved that dress. All the way down to the floor. Off the shoulders. I've always had good shoulders. Your grandfather spoilt me. He'd spoil you if he was alive now.

They ended up in the fountain of the Central Station Hotel.

Him and your father. Dead drunk and singing like lords. They were funny, the pair of them. Their dinner suits all wet and clinging round their ankles. I like a man in a cummerbund. Sitting there in the fountain. Your grandmother, she was that cross. Practically apopleptic. That was the night your father proposed to me, though it was all he could do to remember afterwards. I had witnesses though. I held him to it. I wasn't going to let him get away.

ALAN: You need a necklace.

PEARL: So I do.

ALAN: I'll find you one.

(*He opens up a jewel case – a leather one, with a handle on the top and a key and a lock. He takes out the top tray, with its rings and its cameos.*)

You've fingers like sausages, you. Don't ever wear rings.

PEARL: Thank you.

ALAN: And pearls are for tears.

PEARL: They're all tangled.

ALAN: This is the one.

PEARL: Put it on for me.

(*It's mother-of-pearl shaped into leaves with beads in between.*)

ALAN: Can't reach.

(PEARL *sits down.* ALAN *puts his hands on her shoulders.*)

You're cold.

PEARL: Haven't I been telling you?

ALAN: You're shivering.

PEARL: A goose stepped on my grave.

ALAN: Don't keep saying that.

PEARL: I don't.

ALAN: You do so.

I hate it when you say that.

It's not funny.

What do you say it for?

(*Pause.*)

PEARL: I'm old. I'm getting old.

ALAN: The boys at my school. They think you're my sister.

PEARL: Do they?

ALAN: Yes.

PEARL: Do they really?

ALAN: Yes.

PEARL: Well. Well. Well.

ALAN: Some of them do.

Michael does.

(*Pause.*)

I can probably beat you at arm-wrestling.

PEARL: You probably cannot.

ALAN: I can.

PEARL: Can't.

ALAN: Come on then.

PEARL: In this dress?

ALAN: Warm you up.

PEARL: Not in this dress.

ALAN: Pearl.

PEARL: What?

ALAN: Come on.

(*They get down on to the floor. Lying out at full stretch.*)

PEARL: Oh for God's sake.

ALAN: Best of three.

PEARL: One.

ALAN: Three.

PEARL: One or not at all.

Spit on your hand.

ALAN: What for?

PEARL: Fun, for God's sake.

(*She spits. So does* ALAN.)

ALAN: Other arm behind your back.

PEARL: Why?

ALAN: For fun.

PEARL: Jesus Christ.

(ALAN'*s laughing at her. For blaspheming. For looking funny.*
For trying so hard.)

I'll say what I like.

Don't you laugh at me.

Come on. I'm ready.

I'll beat you.

(*They join hands.*)

39

ALAN: Take the strain.

    Go.

    (*Lightning flashes. Thunder rolls.*

    It's not easy, but PEARL *gets* ALAN's *arm down. She kneels.*

    Dusts herself off.)

PEARL: You're strong. You're growing up.

ALAN: You lifted your elbow.

PEARL: I did not.

    (ALAN *leaps at her, wrestles her down on to the floor.*)

ALAN: You cheated.

PEARL: I don't need to cheat.

    (*Maybe she did. The doubt's there in her mind.*)

ALAN: I wasn't ready.

PEARL: Mind my hair.

ALAN: You wouldn't beat me if I was ready.

PEARL: See that muscle?

    Feel that muscle. Feel it.

    When you've got a muscle like that, then you'll beat me at the arm-wrestling.

ALAN: I hate people like you. (*He's weakening.*) You've always got to win.

    (*She's overpowered him. Lightning. They're quiet now. They stay where they are.*)

    If I asked you to stay.

    (*Thunder.*)

PEARL: It's moving off. I've been counting if you haven't.

ALAN: If I really asked you.

PEARL: What was that?

ALAN: If I asked you and I meant it.

PEARL: There's the gate.

ALAN: Really meant it.

PEARL: Oh my God.

ALAN: Mother.

PEARL: Get up. Get up.

    She'll kill me. Getting her out in this rain. I'm scared of your gran. I've been scared of her all my life. That's a terrible thing, to live in fear of your own mother. And she never lifted a hand to me. Never did. Didn't have to.

        (*Pause.*)
        You'll not ask me to stay.
        (*Pause.*)
        Alan.
        (*Silence.*)
        You'll not ask me.
        (*The doorbell rings.*)
        Your gran's at the door.
        Get up, Alan. Please. Please.
        (*The doorbell rings.*)
        Let your gran in.
ALAN: Mother.
PEARL: Less of your nonsense.
        (*Pause.*)
        I'm going out.
        (*An appeal.*)
        Maybe I love him.
        Maybe I do.
        (*The doorbell's ringing.*)
        On your feet. Alan.
        (*Lightning flash. Clapping rhythm.*)

        (PEARL *smiles a smile like rigor mortis on the stretched mouth of a*
        corpse that died from strychnine poisoning.)
        Oh God.
        Run. Alan, run.
        Don't keep her waiting. Don't for God's sake keep her
        waiting.
        (ALAN *leaves.* PEARL's *in the room. Tidying herself. The*
        bedspread. Frantically.
        Dusting powder off the dressing-table with her hand. Blowing it.
        Wiping her hand on the bedspread. Patting the bedspread.
        Twitching at the curtains. Her hair.
        And all the while VIOLET's *voice comes in from the front door.*
        Starts there and keeps on coming.)
ALAN: Gran.
VIOLET: What have you not got the lights on for? A night like this
        and you've not got the porch light on. Not a welcoming light.

41

There's no harm in a house if there's a bright light shining
for God to see, and that's the truth.

Take my umbrella.

God likes a bright light, and so do I.

Give it a good shaking now before you stack it. I'll have no
pool of water in this hall that your mother can blame me for.

ALAN: She won't mind, my mum.

VIOLET: Do as you're told. I'll hang my own coat up. Thank you.

You shake that well.

Where is she?

ALAN: The bedroom.

VIOLET: Am I to go along a dark hall?

(*She shouts.*)

Pearl.

Am I, Alan?

Put you me that light on.

(*And all the while it's* PEARL *tidying and tidying in the bedroom,
with her mother's voice coming at her from the outside.*

*The hall light goes on and shines into the bedroom. Steps progress
down the hall. And a voice.*)

Listen to that rain. You listen, Alan. There's been some
dirty sins done in the world that God's had to send this much
rain to wash it clean.

(*And she's in the room.*)

Have you not got a lounge you can sit in?

What's up with you?

It's not good for that boy, closeted in here with you, with
your powders and your paints. It's a pansy-man you'll turn
him into. Hurt him for life. I'm telling you. And you'll only
have yourself to blame.

(*She snaps on the main bedroom light. There's only been lamps
before, and the street light from outside shining through the net
curtains.*)

Are you moles, are you, that you're living in the dark? I can't
stand a dark house. Breeds tears, that's what darkness does.
And the sins that come from disappointment. I don't care
what you do when you're on your own, but when I'm coming
you'll have the lights full on.

42

(*And all the while* VIOLET's *tidying the room. Possessing it.*
Twitching the bedspread. The curtains. Shutting a drawer.
Dusting the top of the dressing-table with a hankie.
ALAN's *in the room. They stand and watch* VIOLET, *him and*
PEARL.)
Is that what you're wearing?
(*She surveys her daughter.* PEARL *shrugs.*)
Is it?

PEARL: Yes. Yes. I'm wearing this.

VIOLET: Oh well then.
And your hair?

PEARL: What?

VIOLET: Great long string down your back.

ALAN: I did it.

VIOLET: Eh?

ALAN: I did it, Gran.

VIOLET: And you don't do anything wrong I suppose.
It's up to you what you go out like. It's nothing to do with
me.
Here. (*She gives* ALAN *a notebook and a pen.*) I found that in
your grandfather's desk. Write something he'd be proud of
you for. And here's a postal order I've been saving for you.
And a bag of sweets.
Write me a story.
I've some earrings that I've brought for you. They're good
ones. Pearls. Put them on. I'm past the earring stage. If a
man sees earrings bobbing at your ears he'll know you've still
got joy in your heart.
(*She switches off the bar fire.*)
Light. Light I'll have. It's August. What do you need a fire
for in August? Is there something wrong with your
circulation?

PEARL: No.

VIOLET: For if there's something wrong with your circulation, see
a doctor. Don't waste good money burning heat.
What are you standing there for? Are you going out or aren't
you?

PEARL: Yes.

43

VIOLET: You and this man. This Callum. If this doesn't work . . .

PEARL: Alan's sleeping through here tonight.

VIOLET: What age are you?

PEARL: I said he could.

VIOLET: You're a wee baby, are you?

PEARL: Just for tonight.

VIOLET: You. You spoil him.

Get your coat on.

Why can't you bring him up to be a man? Stand on his own two feet. He'll not do that coorying into his mother's back of a night. God knows what that's teaching him.

PEARL: I've left the tea things.

VIOLET: I can get my own tea.

Why do you not cut your hair?

You'll not fool any man into thinking it's a young bit he's getting. Better to be honest.

You're no spring chicken, my lass, and it's your mother that's saying it.

If this doesn't work with you and Callum. We'll move in together you and me. We'll cut our losses. Two widows together. I didn't speak. Not while there was a chance you'd remarry. There's no point running two establishments. Isn't that right, Alan? (*She doesn't wait for a reply.*) I went straight to the marriage bureau when your father died, Pearl. Straight to the marriage bureau I went. I knew what I wanted and I was going to make damn sure I got it before I was a day older. It's easier living with a man than without. Shut your mouth, Alan. You look gormless.

I know what you're after, my fine lady, though you've left it a bit late. Put your shoes on.

God's a man, I'm telling you. A humorist, that's what God is. A right wee joker. He kills off the men. Gives the women the extra time on the earth to enjoy themselves. A reward for all our labours. But he doesn't leave us the looks to enjoy ourselves with. A right wee joker.

We'll share an establishment you and me.

Cut the costs.

Eh?

44

Then may be you'll have a whole pair of stockings to put to your legs.

(PEARL *snatches her foot up. The one with the stocking with the rip at the toe. And rubs it against the back of her calf..*)

PEARL: I'm thirty-eight years old. My life's not over.

VIOLET: Is that all you are?

(*Pause.*)

Are you going out voluntarily or do I have to shove you out?

PEARL: He's coming for me.

VIOLET: You don't want a man coming in to see this mess. Put him off before he's got right started. You were never much of a housekeeper.

(VIOLET *wipes her finger along the skirting-board. Shows it to her daughter, covered in dust.*)

PEARL: It's not the skirting-boards he's going to be looking at.

VIOLET: Is it not? Is it not then, my fine lady?

Out. Out you go. I've got some pride if you haven't.

(PEARL *goes to kiss* ALAN.)

You let that boy alone. We'll be fine together, him and me. All the better without you slobbering over him.

If you're getting married at the end of this night, well and good.

If not . . .

We'll talk again, you and me.

PEARL: Mother, I . . .

VIOLET: Go on. Go on with you.

Anyone would think you didn't want to go.

PEARL: Night night, Alan.

VIOLET: Aye.

(PEARL *nods to her mother.*)

PEARL: Mum.

(*And she leaves the room. And, as she's leaving, clapping rhythm.*)

(PEARL *walks down the hall to the front door. Heels clacking. Puts on her coat.*

VIOLET *lifts the curtain back. Looks out into the night.*)

VIOLET: Is he there? Is he?

(Her arm goes round ALAN's *shoulder. She pulls him in close. Lifts his face up with hard fingers. Pats his cheek. Fondly, but not gently.*

The rain drives against the window pane. The bright light fades. The lamps are left shining. The boy and the old woman stare out.)

Do you see him?

*(*PEARL *opens the door on to the night.* CALLUM's *standing there in the porch light. He reaches out his hand.)*

CALLUM: Ready?

PEARL: I am.

CALLUM: That's my girl.

PEARL: Ready for anything.

(She laughs up at him. Takes his hand. Crosses the threshold into the night. The street light shines on them.

And the boy and the old woman watching. VIOLET *tapping on the window. Tapping and tapping.*

Clapping rhythm.

Darkness.)

ACT TWO

The Powder Room of a posh hotel.

ALAN's *in his bed in Pearl's room. Asleep with the light on. Just in sight. The revolve almost at full turn but not quite.*

It's late in the evening. The end of the dinner dance. PEARL's *got her coat on. Standing at the mirror in the Powder Room.*

Music there is, at the edge of hearing, coming in from outside the hotel. Rock and roll.

Pearl's humming a different tune. A waltz. Strauss.

She's just washed her hands. Looks up. Catches herself unawares in the glass.

Only PEARL *is lit. Staring straight out at her reflection in the glass.*

PEARL: Look at that face. That's a terrible face. Fancy waking up
every morning to a face like that. What man would want to?
Good God, I don't want to. What's that look in its eye? I
know what you want. I know. You're cheap, that's what you
are. Aye, and you're common too. Do you hear me? Behave
yourself. Go home before you do yourself a damage. You've
drunk too much. And he's drunk too much. Go home before
it ends in tears.
(*She gets close to her reflection in the mirror.*)
You're not listening to me. Don't you come to me with that
face.
That's a night face. That face. A 'come to bed' face. You're
not going out there with a face like that, and you needn't
think it.
I'll fix you.
(*She wipes at her mouth to get the lipstick off. Looks back at the mirror.*)
My God you're bold. Look at those eyes. What are you up
to, eh? Sneaky. What are you going to do, eh? Oh my God.
You'll do it without me. Murky eyes. I don't trust them.
They'll ask for what they want, those eyes. No bother.
I'll fix that face, and you'll not stop me.

47

Anything could happen to a woman that wears a face like that. And none of it nice.

It's an open invitation, that face.

(*She touches the reflection.*)

Don't be too obvious. Never put all your cards on the table at once. Do you hear me? Are you listening to me? No man wants a thing if he thinks it's offered to him on a plate.

(*Snatches her hand away.*)

Take off that face and put a good one on. That's a wicked face. That's the face of a trollop if ever I saw one.

(*She washes her face at the sink. Looks for a towel.*)

Damn.

(*Dries it on the hem of her dress. Looks back at the mirror.*)

All gone.

Pity, eh?

That's your old mum's face. Your goody, goody face. Your 'I know what's good for you' face. Your 'I'm telling you' face. A mother's face. That wee bit tired. Strain round the eyes. A bit wan. That's the face that turns your hair white. Nothing'll happen to that face.

(*She turns away from the mirror. Looks at her watch. Peers at it.*)

You're useless you. Must be late.

I'm that tired. I'm that weary. Home to bed, that's the thing. Straight home. Straight to bed.

Leave the night here. Don't ask for the moon.

(*She peeps back over her shoulder.*)

Who are you kidding? You'll not fool me, and you needn't think it. You're not tired. Not tired at all. You're raring to go, you.

(*Takes a decision. Slashes lipstick at her mouth.*)

We'll go halfway. We've some fun left in us yet, and why not? Our life's not over. We've the world in front of us. A halfway face. It can take its chance. A 'maybe maybe' face. A bit of lipstick. There's no harm. Nun's eyes and a harlot's mouth. We'll leave it to him. Choice. What do you say, face? He can take his choice.

We'll not tell him what we want. Keep him guessing. Eh, face?

48

(*Touches her harlot's lips. Clapping rhythm.*)

(*The lights widen out.* PEARL's *standing at the end of the
ballroom.
The lights beam bright in the ballroom. The chandeliers twinkle
and shine. The glass tinkles as a breeze blows through the place.
Music's coming in on the wind. Rock and roll from the jukebox at
full belt in the café across the road. The curtains on the ballroom
windows are wide open, and the lights of the café across the road
shine in.
There are tables in the ballroom. Large round ones in the empty
ballroom, with the ruination of a good meal upon them. And
streamers strewn round.* CALLUM *leans up against one table,
overcoat over dinner suit, arms folded, patiently waiting. Eight
empty chairs sit there higgledy-piggledy. Bottles of wine half-
drunk.
There's a floral decoration in the middle of each table. Built on a
circle it is, and made of white Madonna lilies and dark
evergreen.*
PEARL's *got her dark coat on over her dance dress. Just an edge
of the dress kicks out. A piece of coral flame.
The music's louder in the ballroom.*)

PEARL: Oh God. I didn't mean to be last. Are we the last? Have I
kept you?

CALLUM: Not at all.

PEARL: I have. I've kept you.

CALLUM: Not to speak of.

PEARL: I haven't kept you too long?

CALLUM: Doesn't signify.

PEARL: You're sure?

CALLUM: Pearl!
(*He's smiling. Teasing.*)
I'd wait for ever if I had to.

PEARL: That's an awful long time, and no reward at the end of it.
You'd not wait gladly.

CALLUM: I'd wait.

PEARL: You would not.

CALLUM: I'd wait all right.

(*He puts his arm round her.*)

PEARL: The wind in here.

CALLUM: The doors are open.

PEARL: They must want rid of us. They've their warm beds
waiting for them. Sorry.

CALLUM: What for?

PEARL: I was so long.

CALLUM: For God's sake, Pearl.

(*Pause.* PEARL's *smiling at him. Touching his cheek. One finger
lightly touching his cheekbone. Running along it.*)

PEARL: Pity they have to end.

CALLUM: What?

PEARL: Nice times.

CALLUM: Nothing's ending.

(*The music floats on.*)

PEARL: Kids'll be dancing. Across the street they'll be dancing.
Makes you feel old. Makes me feel old anyway.

CALLUM: You'll never be old.

PEARL: Will I not then?

CALLUM: Not ever.

PEARL: Well then?

(*She's smiling. Still in his arms. Then* CALLUM *leaps away from
her.*)

CALLUM: Want a dance?

PEARL: Don't be daft.

CALLUM: I want to dance.

PEARL: Do you now?

CALLUM: I do.

PEARL: Is that right?

CALLUM: Come on.

PEARL: I've my coat on.

CALLUM: Take it off.

PEARL: I've done my dancing this fine evening.

CALLUM: Hey.

PEARL: Hay's for horses.

CALLUM: Come for a gallop.

(*He sashays out on to the floor. Exercises a quick combination of
cross-legged steps. Ends with a twirl. Throws off his coat.*)

Hay!
(PEARL's clapping and laughing. CALLUM's back at her, unbuttoning her coat.)
We're dancing, you and me.

PEARL: Callum.

(CALLUM kisses her throat.)

CALLUM: You've fine skin.

PEARL: Have I?

(CALLUM's whirling away from her again.)

CALLUM: See me. I'm the jitterbug king.

(He's laughing at her.)

PEARL: Is that right?

CALLUM: It is. Diamonds in your eyes.

PEARL: Get away with you.

CALLUM: Trouble with you is . . .

PEARL: What?

CALLUM: Trouble with you . . .

PEARL: Eh?

CALLUM: You don't know how to take a compliment.

PEARL: I do. I . . .

CALLUM: 'Thank you.' Say.

PEARL: I like compliments.

CALLUM: 'Thank you very much.'

PEARL: Any old compliment'll do.

CALLUM: And cast down your eyes.

PEARL: I can take all the compliments you can give me.

CALLUM: Did your mother not teach you anything?

PEARL: Never trust a flatterer, that's what she taught me. But I didn't listen.

CALLUM: We're going to try again.

PEARL: Don't be . . .

CALLUM: Will we try again?

PEARL: Yes.

CALLUM: 'Yes please.'

(PEARL smiles at him.)

PEARL: Please.

CALLUM: You've fine skin. *(He kisses her shoulder.)*

PEARL: Thank you.

CALLUM: Skin like velvet.

PEARL: Don't be daft.

CALLUM: Ah!

PEARL: Sorry. Sorry. I'm sorry.
Say something else.

CALLUM: That's your lot.

PEARL: Something else nice.

CALLUM: You'll get spoilt.

PEARL: I'd like that.

CALLUM: Listen to that music.

PEARL: I should go.

CALLUM: You're staying.

PEARL: I should go home.

CALLUM: You're staying here with me.

PEARL: My lovely evening . . .

CALLUM: Listen.

PEARL: It's gone so fast.

CALLUM: You're not listening.

PEARL: It's loud enough.

CALLUM: Sets your foot tapping. Eh?

PEARL: Folks round here.

CALLUM: What?

PEARL: They'll be calling in the police.
(CALLUM *whisks open his jacket*.)

CALLUM: Feel my heart.

PEARL: You've had too much to drink.

CALLUM: A good thing too.

PEARL: Your heart's thumping.

CALLUM: We're dancing, you and me.

PEARL: Never ask for more.

CALLUM: Eh?

PEARL: If you're greedy, God'll punish you.

CALLUM: Is that what you teach your son?
(*He unties his bow tie*.)

PEARL: It's true.
Never ask for more.
They'll get you.

CALLUM: Who will?

PEARL: I've had a wonderful evening.

CALLUM: We'll go right into the night, you and me. That's what we'll do. God and all his angels'll not stop us. For I'll not let them.

(*He's down to his braces.*)

PEARL: You look . . .

CALLUM: What?

PEARL: I like a man in braces.

CALLUM: I like a woman that knows what she likes.

(*He holds out his hand to her. And the music's playing.*)

PEARL: I'm a fox-trot lady, me.

CALLUM: Not tonight.

(*Then PEARL's close to him.*)

We'll dare tonight.

PEARL: I love the nape of your neck.

CALLUM: Eh?

PEARL: There. There where I'm touching you.

CALLUM: You've cold fingers.

PEARL: And your eyelashes.

(*She's close to him. Arms around him.*)

CALLUM: Are you laughing at me?

PEARL: Why do the men always have the eyelashes?

CALLUM: I'll teach you to laugh at me.

PEARL: Have you put vaseline on them?

CALLUM: Cheeky wee . . .

(*He pulls her on to the dance floor.*)

PEARL: The way they shine. Don't you tell me that's natural. You've vaseline on them. You have.

CALLUM: I'll teach you.

(*He breaks away from her.*)

Come here. Come on. Right here. I'm waiting.

PEARL: Bide your patience. I'll be there in my own good time.

CALLUM: You're wicked you.

(*He holds out his hand.*)

PEARL: Am I?

CALLUM: Aye, you are.

PEARL: Not wicked enough.

CALLUM: That's the drink talking.

PEARL: Aye, and it's the drink dancing and that's a fact.

(*She joins him on the dance floor.* CALLUM *pulls her into a jive full of twirls. Lifts her up. Holds her. Sets her down on the floor. Faintly, under the music, there's a clapping rhythm getting louder and louder.*)

I'm out of breath.

Callum.

I can't.

I can't dance anymore.

(*There's only the clapping rhythm. The music changes – 'The Twelfth of Never'. They're panting, the two of them.*)

PEARL: I'm sweating.

CALLUM: Sh. Sh. Sh. Sh.

PEARL: A woman of my age.

CALLUM: Sh. Sh. Sh.

(*They dance close.* PEARL *joins in with the song. Breathless at first. Then full-voiced. Teasing him.*)

PEARL: Hold me close,

Never let me go;

Hold me close,

Melt my heart like April snow.

I love . . . hmmm mmm mmmm mmmmm mmm hmmmm hmmm.

I love you till the roses have lost their sweet perfume.

I love you till the poet's run out of rhyme

Until the Twelfth of Never,

And that's a long, long time.

CALLUM: You're wicked.

PEARL: Once in my life . . .

CALLUM: What?

PEARL: I'd like to do what I want.

CALLUM: What's that?

(*Pause.*)

What do you want?

PEARL: The moon from out of the sky. Will you get it for me?

CALLUM: Now?

PEARL: Don't be daft.

CALLUM: What do you really want?

PEARL: I told you.

(There's screams from across the road. Cries of excitement. The music changes back to a jive again.)

PEARL: I've got to go.

CALLUM: Nonsense.

PEARL: Callum.

CALLUM: One more dance.

PEARL: I'm late.

CALLUM: I love you.

PEARL: How can you love me? You don't know me.

('Wake up Little Susie')

Somebody likes that song.

CALLUM: I don't know you?

PEARL: No.

CALLUM: Don't I?

PEARL: No.

CALLUM: I don't know you.

PEARL: You don't.

CALLUM: What is it then?

PEARL: What?

CALLUM: What is it?

PEARL: Eh?

CALLUM: What do I not know?

PEARL: Callum.

CALLUM: You tell me.

PEARL: Tell you what?

CALLUM: Tell me.

PEARL: What?

CALLUM: I'm asking you.

PEARL: What do you mean?

CALLUM: I'm asking.

PEARL: Stop it, Callum.

CALLUM: Would you cheat me?

PEARL: I don't know what you mean. *(This trying to laugh.)*

CALLUM: Would you?

(Twirling her and twirling her.)

PEARL: I'm dizzy.

(In and out. Pulled to and fro. Skirts flying out and wide.

55

CALLUM's *slapping one hand against his thigh. It makes a clapping sound.*)

CALLUM: Come on.

PEARL: Stop it.

CALLUM: Come on now.

PEARL: Stop.

CALLUM: Whisper.

PEARL: I'm old for this game.

CALLUM: I'll keep your secrets.

PEARL: Callum.

CALLUM: Tell me.

PEARL: I'm out of breath.

(CALLUM's *got her in both arms and he's swinging her round.*)
I've nothing to tell.
It's an ordinary life, my life.
That's the truth.

CALLUM: Not so.

PEARL: You're daft.

CALLUM: I want . . .

PEARL: What? What?

CALLUM: Your husband.

PEARL: My husband?

CALLUM: Tell me. Come on. Come on.

PEARL: Someone'll hear.

CALLUM: Let them.

PEARL: What do you want? I don't know what you want. What game is it we're playing, Callum? I don't know.
I'm dizzy.

CALLUM: Your husband, Pearl. Tell me about him.

(CALLUM *stops twirling her. Grabs her in close.*)
You haven't a picture of him in your house.

PEARL: I don't need one.

CALLUM: Not a photograph.

PEARL: What am I to tell?
Please?

(CALLUM's *got his hands on the sides of her head. Turning her round in a slow circle. Keeping her moving. His hands press tight. Not hurting. Tight enough.*)

56

CALLUM: What did you call him?

PEARL: Thomas.

CALLUM: I know his name. Tom? Tommy? What did you call him?

PEARL: I like you, Callum. Please.

(CALLUM's *still turning her round. Still with his hands at the sides of her head.*)

CALLUM: And I love you.

PEARL: Do you?

CALLUM: You hear me?

PEARL: You love me?

Tom I called him.

Can we stop this now?

CALLUM: Tom. Tom did you call him in your private moments. Tom?

PEARL: Yes. Yes.

CALLUM: You've never spoken of him.

PEARL: It's a difficult subject to broach.

CALLUM: I'd've listened. Any time. Pearl. Not once. Told me nothing of him. Pearl. Made a ghost of him to haunt me with. Made him perfection that I have to compete with. First thing that comes into your head.

PEARL: Please let me go.

CALLUM: Come on. Come on. Tell me.

PEARL: You let me go. (*She's commanding him.*)

CALLUM: Is that how you talk to your son? Do you bully your son? Won't work with me.

PEARL: I'm tired.

CALLUM: Don't give me that.

PEARL: What?

CALLUM: I see the look in your eye.

PEARL: What?

CALLUM: I know what you want.

PEARL: Do you?

CALLUM: You're not tired.

PEARL: Please.

CALLUM: Come on now. Tom.

PEARL: I should have gone home.

57

CALLUM: Now. First thing. First thing.
(*He's holding her very tight.*)
It's a game, Pearl. That's all.
PEARL: Is that what it is?
Is it?
What kind of a game?
Someone'll come.
Please. What's the rules of this game?
CALLUM: You'll not cheat me.
PEARL: VJ Day.
CALLUM: Go on. Go on. Don't stop dancing.
PEARL: My feet are killing me.
CALLUM: VJ Day.
PEARL: I don't like this game. I don't want to remember things.
What's the use? I'm always having to remember. Pulling
things out. For Alan. For you. What use is the past to me?
Eh? What use is it?
CALLUM: You're shaking like a leaf.
PEARL: I'm cold.
CALLUM: I haven't hurt you.
PEARL: No, you haven't hurt me. I'm not a wee girl.
(*Pause.*
She looks at him. Puts her hands on his. Pulls them away. Holds
them. They're still, the pair of them.)
PEARL: We were in the town.
CALLUM: Yes?
PEARL: Staying.
I've my life together. Me and Alan.
CALLUM: You've done well.
PEARL: I fought to get my life together. I'm going to keep it that
way.
CALLUM: I'm part of your life now.
PEARL: What if you don't like what I tell you? Will I lose you?
Will I?
CALLUM: There now. There. There. There.
(*He cradles her in his arms.*)
VJ Day. I'm listening. You were in the town. Staying. You
and Tom. Tommy did you call him? Precious moments.

58

Quiet moments. Did you never call him Tommy? Come on
Pearl. Come on. Come on. Come on. Come on. In the town
. . . In the town . . .

PEARL: There was a noise.

CALLUM: What noise? What?

PEARL: I'm telling you.

CALLUM: What kind of noise?

PEARL: I'll tell it in my own way.

CALLUM: Was it dark?

PEARL: Very dark. There's no dark now like there was then. Let
this be.

CALLUM: There was a noise. The noise? The noise?

PEARL: Let's just be you and me, without the shadows. I don't
ask you about your women. I don't want to know. You're
you and you're here and that's what matters. You must have
had women. They're nothing to me.

CALLUM: What was the noise?

PEARL: We were in the town. We were staying. We were in bed.
We were young. We were in bed early. In the distance. Far
distance. There was this noise.

CALLUM: Quiet now. Hush.

(*He's smoothing her hair.*)

There's my good girl. My good, good girl.

PEARL: Didn't know what it was. Neither one of us. Getting
louder. The noise. I'm clinging to him. Louder and louder.
Coming down on us. He leaps for the window. Flings the
damn thing open. The noise floods in. All through the room
it goes. Till I've got my hands over my ears to keep the damn
noise out of my head. 'Tom. Tom.' I'm shouting for I'm
terrified. And he's laughing. 'Come here,' he's shouting. His
voice fills the whole room. And the outside clatter. And he's
pulling my hands down from my ears. And he gets me to the
window. And I'm afraid. Of him. For he's laughing and
laughing. And it's everywhere, this damn noise. Then I see
them. He's making me see them. The girls it is. Running
down the hill. Over the cobbles. Down the hill. The noise of
their hard shoes on the cobblestones. The clatter. Hundreds
of them. The late shift from the jute mills. Running and

running down the hills to the town square. And it lights up as I'm looking. Lights everywhere. The war's over. And we went to bed, him and me, and for joy we made a baby.

(CALLUM's *holding her by the tops of her arms.*)

Tommy. Tommy.

(*Pause.*)

CALLUM: I've drunk more than I thought.

(*He lets her go.*)

I beg your pardon.

(*The lights dim.*)

They want us out.

PEARL: Damn breeze in here.

Listen.

(*A police siren. Shouting. The music's stopped.*)

Pulled the plug out.

Stay in your own house, that's what I say. Safe and sound.

(*The lights across the road go out.*)

What harm were they doing with their music?

(*She shakes at the watch on her wrist.*)

It's late.

(CALLUM *drapes her coat round her shoulders.*)

Thank you.

(*She kisses him.* CALLUM *doesn't put his arms round her.*)

It's awful quiet.

(CALLUM *watches her.*)

Callum?

(*Silence. The music's gone. And the shouting. There's only the tinkling of the chandeliers left.*

CALLUM *ties his tie. Puts on his jacket. Buttons it. His coat. While she chatters. For she doesn't like the silence.*)

Size of a pocket handkerchief this dance floor. For a party this size. Where have I not had elbows? I'm covered in bruises. Not that I've not had a nice night. I've had a lovely night.

(*Every time she stops talking, the silence crowds in on her again.*)

Thank you.

And for my flower.

(*There's an orchid pinned to her dress. She fiddles with the Madonna lilies on the table as she's speaking. Smooths a lily*

from base to curled petal tip. Picks one up.)
Six would have been a better number at these tables.
(CALLUM's *buttoning his coat.*)
Nice dinner, mind. Nice, nice dinner. Pity about the steak.
As well we've both got our own teeth. The man next to me
had a terrible tussle. And the vegetables. They were asking
for swimming lessons, the vegetables.
As for the fresh fruit salad. Call that fresh fruit? Guy funny
tree. The tree that bore that fruit.
And cream? Cream?
If that ever saw the inside of a cow it wasnie the kind of a cow
I call a cow.
Laugh. Go on. For God's sake laugh.
Call it by a fancy French name and you can get away with
anything. My son, he'll speak French one day. One day he'll
speak French.

CALLUM: Ready?
       (*The lights blink.*)
PEARL: I'd like to walk back home. Would you mind? Get the air
       to my face. The rain's stopped. A bit of fresh air. Before I see
       my mother.
CALLUM: Of course.
       (PEARL *looks at him.*)
PEARL: Champagne. It's all promises. Eh?
       (*Clapping rhythm.*)

       (PEARL's *carrying the lilies from the table. The ballroom drifts
       away from them. They're journeying, the pair of them. Stars
       twinkle.*
       *Lights of passing cars shine on them as they travel. And the sound
       of cars too. A few.*
       PEARL *picks at the flowers so the petals trail out behind her.*
       CALLUM *catches at her hand.*)
CALLUM: Let it be.
PEARL: What?
CALLUM: What did it ever . . .
PEARL: Eh?
CALLUM: Poor bloody flower.

61

Spent all that time growing for you to spread it out in the puddles.

(*Pause.*)

PEARL: Were you . . .

CALLUM: What?

PEARL: Curiosity killed the cat, they say.

CALLUM: So they do.

PEARL: See the light? That's my house. My very own.

CALLUM: It's a nice house.

PEARL: Do you like it? Do you really like it?

CALLUM: Very much.

PEARL: My mother's there tonight, staying.
Callum.

CALLUM: What?

PEARL: Was there something you were going to ask me?

(*Beat.*)

CALLUM: Not that I know of.

(*Pause.*)

PEARL: You're not the first man to come chapping at my door.

CALLUM: Don't, Pearl.

PEARL: Not by a long chalk. There's many a many come chapping at my door.

CALLUM: You're a lovely woman.

PEARL: There'll be many a many yet.

CALLUM: That's right.

PEARL: I should think so.

CALLUM: I'm sorry.

PEARL: What on earth are you sorry for? Good Lord. There's nothing you've got to apologize to me for.
I've a good job.

CALLUM: I know you have.

PEARL: The job I've got . . .

CALLUM: I never said . . .

PEARL: I dress the women in this town. I've a good eye. I dress them. The good women. Not the posh ones. The ones that know where they're going. That's who I dress. And they're going there on their own. God help them. That's who I dress. Suits I buy in for them. I'm telling you. Business suits they're wearing, the women now.

I cook. I cook well.

'I love you.' Did you say that to me?

CALLUM: No.

PEARL: No?

CALLUM: Pearl . . .

PEARL: No, you didn't, did you? I don't suppose you did.

And document cases they're buying too, for their work. To carry it in. I've made a good life for my son.

Feel the nap on this coat.

Come you here and feel this.

Have a feel of this.

(CALLUM *does*.)

CALLUM: It's a nice coat.

PEARL: It's my triumph, this coat. I count my triumphs. It's a damn good coat, this coat. And I bought it and I paid for it. And this dress. It's my only dance dress. But you see the label on this. I'm a triumph standing here. That's what I am.

CALLUM: You'd make any man proud to . . .

PEARL: Will you marry me?

(*Pause*.)

Don't say anything. I perfectly understand. Any explanation would be superfluous.

(*Pause*.)

I can see the house from here. There's really no need for you to come any further.

CALLUM: I'll see you to the door.

PEARL: The porch light's shining. There really is no need. I'm quite capable of looking after myself.

(*She holds out her hand for him to shake it*.)

CALLUM: You're a beautiful woman.

PEARL: Next time I'm born I'll be a man.

CALLUM: You'd not make a very good one.

PEARL: I just need to be taller, that's all I need.

(*Pause*.)

Thank you for a pleasant evening.

CALLUM: My pleasure.

PEARL: I'll say goodnight.

CALLUM: Pearl, I . . .

PEARL: Feel that wind. Blowing and blowing. Summer's over.
Pity. Eh?

I'd ask you in for a nightcap. But Alan's in my bedroom and
my mum's on the sofa in the lounge. A sherry to us standing
up in the hall, that's all that's left.

Not very exciting.

Goodnight, then.

Eh?

CALLUM: Goodnight, Pearl.

(*Then hugging herself, for the wind's blowing,* PEARL *watches
him go. Even after he's gone she watches. Whispers.*)

PEARL: The touch of you. The feel of your skin. Your eyes
looking at me. Your arms holding me. Surprise of you.
Smooth skin. Touch of velvet.

(*Pause.*)

The strength of you. Holding me. Taking the breath out of
me. Scent of you.

(*There's a smile on her face.*

Clapping rhythm.)

(*The home crowds back in on* PEARL, *slowly.*

The lamp's on in her room

ALAN *turns over in his sleep. Leaps out of bed. Feels himself.*

*Bends down and feels the bed. Grabs his dressing-gown. Runs to
the bathroom.*

Back in the room. PEARL's *still got her coat on.* ALAN's *wet the
bed. She gets the sheets stripped off,* PEARL, *and she lifts up the
mattress, hauls at it to get it turned. It's not easy.*

ALAN *comes in from the bathroom.*)

PEARL: Did you dry yourself properly?

Don't just look at me.

Grab a hold of this. I'm breaking my nails.

Did your gran hear you?

ALAN: No.

PEARL: Are you sure?

ALAN: Yes.

(*He tries to help. Fingers grasp at the sides of the mattress and*

64

wrench off.)

PEARL: Oh for God's sake.

Sit there till I'm finished.

(ALAN *gets in her way*.)

Sit by the fire.

(ALAN *switches the fire on*.)

ALAN: The water was cold.

PEARL: Serves you right.

I hope you washed properly. You'll stink if you didn't, and all the boys at school'll know exactly what it is you stink of.

ALAN: Mother.

PEARL: Don't whine. Don't for God's sake whine.

ALAN: Don't be angry.

PEARL: I'm not angry.

(*She's catching at her breath*.)

ALAN: You are.

PEARL: Eh?

ALAN: You are so.

(PEARL *lets the mattress fall into place. Sits down, out of breath*.)

PEARL: Oh God, I forgot to bring you anything. Alan, I didn't bring you anything.

(*Starts to sob. Then she can't stop*.)

I'm an awful fool.

ALAN: No you're not.

PEARL: I open my mouth and the words come tumbling out and I can't stop them and they're never the right words and I wish they were. Oh Alan, I wish they were.

(ALAN *doesn't know what to do. Then he does. He puts his arms around her*.)

PEARL: I haven't a hankie.

(ALAN *takes one out of his dressing-gown pocket*.)

How long's that been there?

(*But she takes it*.)

I've told you to clear out your pockets. Look at the state of it.

(*Blows her nose*.)

You never listen to a word I say.

(*Sniffs*.)

You clear out your pockets once a week so I can get the

washing done properly. Do you hear me?

(*Bursts into sobs again.* ALAN *pats her shoulder.*)

ALAN: Stop it.

PEARL: Alan.

ALAN: Gran'll hear.

(*Patting and patting.*)

Please stop it.

PEARL: Don't keep patting me. I'm not a dog.

ALAN: Is there something wrong with you?

PEARL: Of course there's something wrong with me.

ALAN: What?

PEARL: Would I be blubbering if something wasn't wrong?

ALAN: Well?

PEARL: Well, what are you asking me for?

ALAN: Did you not have a nice time?

PEARL: What do you think?

ALAN: I don't know.

PEARL: Your father should never have left me.

ALAN: He couldn't help it.

PEARL: Oh yes he could.

He did it deliberately.

ALAN: Mother.

PEARL: He didn't say goodbye. Not a word. I'd have said
goodbye if it had been me.

ALAN: Mother.

PEARL: I would. I would so. If I was going to die I'd do it
properly. Not go off half-cock. Toes in the air. Trousers
round my knees on a bathroom floor. At thirty-five years old.
People don't die at thirty-five years old.

Always say goodbye, Alan. Finish things off.

I'm good at my job.

ALAN: I know you are.

PEARL: Maybe I'll travel, one day, when you're older. Maybe
they'll send me to the Paris fashion shows one day. They
might, Alan. Sure they might. I want to be someone. Alan.
There's nothing wrong with that. I can be someone. You
don't just have a child and your life's over. I'll be someone
yet. You watch. You watch me.

66

ALAN: Did he ask you?

PEARL: I don't want a man. Not any man.

ALAN: Didn't he ask you?

PEARL: In the big wide world that's all opening up just for me I'll be someone.

ALAN: He didn't ask you.

PEARL: Of course he asked me. He asked me all right. Don't you worry. What do you think I am. I made damn sure he asked me.

ALAN: Well then?

PEARL: Take that look off your face.

ALAN: Well?

PEARL: It wasn't a good enough offer.

Don't look at me. Turn your eyes away.

I said no. Not for you. So you needn't think it. For me I said no. For my own self. And you remember that, for it's the truth I'm telling you. Tonight. In years to come I might say something different. Who knows? I might even blame you. For I'll be alone. Or I'll be with your gran, and that'll be worse. And I like men. Most of the time. Right now I could see them far enough. I like a man's arms around me. I like all of it. Even sex I like. Oh yes I do. And don't you look like that. You know very well what goes on between a man and a woman in a bed. And I know you know.

(*Pause.*)

If I hurt, I'll lash out at whatever comes nearest. You remember that. Will you?

ALAN: Yes.

PEARL: Don't just 'Yes' me.

ALAN: I want to go back to bed.

PEARL: Were you listening? I said no to him for I don't need a man. I'm on my own, and that suits me fine. D'you hear?

ALAN: Come on to bed.

PEARL: You hear what suits you. How could he not ask me? I don't come empty-handed.

(*She's down at the bar fire. Still with her coat on.*)

ALAN: I'm awful tired.

PEARL: What do you think I am?

67

(They both work on the bed. Taking the clean sheets from the big bottom drawer of the dressing-table.)

ALAN: Mother.

PEARL: Eh?

ALAN: Can I ask you something?

PEARL: Ask away. Asking's free.

ALAN: You know the pictures?

PEARL: Eh?

ALAN: Give me the money to go on my own on Saturday.

PEARL: What?

ALAN: Give me the money to go with David.
Mother?

PEARL: Aren't we going together?

ALAN: It's a cowboy.

PEARL: I don't mind.

ALAN: I want to go with David. Can I? Brian'll be going and all of them. Mother. Please. And can we have our tea in the cafeteria? Me and David. It'll not cost any more than if you and me went.

PEARL: Haven't you some friend from your own school you can go with? Michael?

ALAN: I like David better.

PEARL: I'm not saying he's not nice. He's old for you. Someone your own age, son.
What'll the waitresses think? The pair of you alone together.

ALAN: We'll behave ourselves. Can we go? Mother. Please. Can we?

PEARL: Of course.

ALAN: What are you smiling like that for?

PEARL: Go by all means. If that's what you want.

ALAN: Mother?

PEARL: Go on your own. The pair of you.

ALAN: You don't mind?

PEARL: Provided your homework's done on Friday night. And no fuss. Do you hear me?

ALAN: You really don't mind? Really?
(Of course she does.)

PEARL: Tuck that sheet in tight.

68

I don't want to see an old cowboy film. What do I want to go out with a boy for?

They're all the same. Cowboys, horses. I don't like horses. And some wet woman with big eyes mawking about the place.

ALAN: Don't smile like that.

PEARL: You go. The pair of you. I've a book from the library. I'll put my feet up.

ALAN: Stop smiling.

PEARL: Nurse my varicose veins. I'll have my tea on a tray by the fire. Winter's coming. I've had my night out. After all.

(*She holds the bedcover up for him to get in.*)

ALAN: You haven't got any varicose veins.

PEARL: I had them once. When I was carrying you. I can get them again. I'm a glorified shop-girl, after all. Isn't that what they get, shop-girls? Varicose veins?

(*She's still smiling.*)

ALAN: What's so funny?

PEARL: Here.

(*She unpins the flower from her dress and lays it on the pillow. ALAN touches the petals. Smooths them from stamen to curled petal tip.*)

ALAN: Don't be long.

PEARL: I won't.

(*She touches his cheek. Wanders over to the window. Peeps out from the curtains. Stands with her coat on looking out into the night.*)

Light's still on. Someone's having a good time.

(*She sits down at the dressing-table and pins her hair up for the night. Creams her face to get the make-up off. Puts her hand out to touch her reflection.*)

We're old for nights like this. You and me.

(*She's laughing at herself.*)

Next time we see him. He'll be pushing a pram in the park with some other woman's brat in it. That's when we'll see him. If ever a man was ripe for marriage. Dying for it.

(*She takes the top off the cream jar. Covers her face with white cream.*)

Her mother's voice comes to her from the lounge.)

VIOLET: Is that you, dear?

PEARL: Yes.

VIOLET: Are you back?

PEARL: Did I wake you?

VIOLET: Did you have a nice time?

PEARL: Yes.

VIOLET: Eh?

PEARL: I had a very nice time.

(*The cream's all over her face.*)

VIOLET: That's good then. That's very good.

(*Clapping rhythm.*)

(ALAN's *eyes are closed.*

PEARL *wipes at her face with a piece of cotton wool. Gets up and throws open the window. Leans on the window-sill, breathing in the air.*

The curtains blow. ALAN *stirs.*)

ALAN: Mother?

PEARL: Shhhh.

ALAN: What are you doing?

PEARL: Letting in the air for God's sake. I'm letting in the air.

(*And the lights dip down and into darkness.*)